Maria Sharapova

Revised Edition

By Jeff Savage

Lerner Publications Company • Minneapolis

Copyright © 2014 by Jeff Savage

All rights reserved. International copyright secured. No part of this book may be reproduced, stored in a retrieval system, or transmitted in any form or by any means—electronic, mechanical, photocopying, recording, or otherwise—without the prior written permission of Lerner Publishing Group, Inc., except for the inclusion of brief quotations in an acknowledged review.

Lerner Publications Company
A division of Lerner Publishing Group, Inc.
241 First Avenue North
Minneapolis, MN 55401 USA

For reading levels and more information, look up this title at www.lernerbooks.com.

Library of Congress Cataloging-in-Publication Data

Savage, Jeff, 1961– author.
    Maria Sharapova / by Jeff Savage. — Revised edition.
        pages   cm — (Amazing athletes)
    Includes index.
    ISBN 978–1–4677–2643–6 (pbk. : alk. paper)
    ISBN 978–1–4677–2644–3 (eBook)
    1. Sharapova, Maria, 1987–—Juvenile literature. 2. Tennis players—Russia (Federation)—Biography—Juvenile literature. 3. Women tennis players—Russia (Federation)—Biography—Juvenile literature. I. Title.
    GV994.S28S27 2014
    796.342092—dc23 [B]   2013022639

Manufactured in the United States of America
1 – BP – 12/31/13

TABLE OF CONTENTS

Maria hits the ball to Sara Errani at the 2012 French Open.

FRENCH CHAMP

Russian tennis player Maria Sharapova stood near the **baseline**. She bounced the ball twice and looked across the court at Sara Errani. Maria tossed the ball in the air and swung her racket. The ball streaked over the net as she let out a scream that echoed through the stadium.

The **serve** sailed past Errani before the young Italian could react. Another **ace** for Maria!

Maria and Errani were playing against each other in the **final** match of the 2012 French Open in Paris, France. The stadium was full of excited fans. TV cameras captured every move. The winner would be named champion of the **tournament**.

Maria played in front of a very large crowd at the 2012 French Open.

Maria always gives her best effort on the tennis court.

Both players were 25 years old at the time. But Maria had a lot more experience in big matches. She had already won three of the four **Grand Slam** women's tennis tournaments in past years.

The four Grand Slam tennis tournaments are the US Open, the Australian Open, the French Open, and Wimbledon.

Sara Errani serves to Maria at the 2012 French Open.

Only nine women in history have won all four Grand Slams in their careers. If Maria could win the French Open, she would be the 10th.

Maria was ready when Errani prepared to serve. The tall Russian is great at hitting **returns**. No one in the world does it better. When the ball came toward her, Maria returned it with power. Errani could not catch up.

Maria took the first **set**, 6–3. Then she took the lead in the second set, 5–2. When Errani hit a **backhand** into the net, the match was over. Maria had won the French Open!

She sank to her knees on the court. She raised both arms in victory as the crowd stood and cheered. Winning all four Grand Slams had been a long journey for Maria. But the hard work was worth it. "It's the most unique moment I've experienced in my career," she said.

Maria celebrating after her big win.

When Maria was three years old, her parents moved from Siberia to Sochi *(above)*. The town lies in southwestern Russia.

A TOUGH START

Maria was born April 19, 1987, to Yuri and Yelena Sharapova. Her family lived in Siberia, a large region within Russia. Yuri was a construction worker. Yelena stayed home to raise Maria, their only child.

Yuri became friends with the father of Yevgeny Kafelnikov, a Russian **professional** tennis player. In 1991, Kafelnikov's father gave Maria a tennis racket as a gift. She practiced hitting tennis balls against the side of her house. In 1993, when Maria was six, her father took her to a children's tennis clinic in Moscow, the Russian capital. Martina Navratilova, a great female tennis player, was there. She saw Maria

Martina Navratilova *(below)* is a tennis legend.

hitting balls. "She has talent," Navratilova told Maria's father.

Yuri decided to get expert coaching for Maria. In 1995, he packed up a few belongings and flew with Maria to the United States. In Bradenton, Florida, he took her to the Nick Bollettieri Tennis Academy. The school was famous for training many stars, including Andre Agassi and Monica Seles. "In the beginning it was tough to tell how good she was," Coach Bollettieri said. Eventually, though, Maria got into the academy. Yuri had to work several jobs to pay her **tuition**.

Yuri and Maria came to the United States with little money. Neither spoke English. They had to ride several buses to reach the tennis academy. Maria didn't get into the academy right away.

Maria and her father *(left)* are very close.

Maria lived in a **dormitory** with older girls. Yuri moved into an apartment one mile away. The family couldn't afford to buy a car. So Yuri walked to work and to see Maria every day. Maria's mother stayed in Russia until she could get the paperwork that let her come to America.

Maria went to school at the academy. She spoke little English. Her speech was awkward.

The other students teased her. She was especially lonely at the dormitory. "I had only myself as company," she said.

Maria worked hard at tennis. She was tall for her age. So she struggled to keep her balance and smooth movement on the court. The other girls bullied her. "It just made me tougher," she said. Maria's **agent**, Max Eisenbud, remembers how hard it was for Maria and her father. "Yuri calls it survival," Eisenbud said. "It was two very tough years. They don't forget what it was like."

Coach Nick Bollettieri *(right)* poses with Maria before a match.

GOLDEN GIRL

Over time, Maria blossomed as a tennis player. In 1996, when she was nine years old, the academy began paying her tuition. She started competing in junior tennis events. In 1997, Maria played in the Eddie Herr International

Junior Championships for kids 14 and under. She beat a strong player named Bernice Burlet, 6–3, 6–4. Maria was only 10 years old!

A year later, she joined the International Management Group (IMG). IMG would represent her in any tennis deals. In exchange, Maria got free shoes and tennis rackets.

At the same time, Maria started traveling to Southern California for lessons from famed coach Robert Lansdorp. "I would get bored after hitting four balls in a row in one corner, and he made me hit 100," said Maria. "He taught me patience and consistency and drive."

Maria plays tennis right-handed. But she is a natural lefty. When she was 10 years old, she started playing left-handed. After six months, she switched back.

Daily practice lasted six hours. The hard work paid off. Maria won tournaments often.

The tennis world was learning about this spaghetti-thin girl with the powerful game and fierce desire.

Starting in March 2001, Maria grew quickly. In one year, she sprouted from five foot three inches to five foot nine! Maria became the youngest-ever girls' finalist at the Australian Open Junior Championship. She swept through the first four rounds without losing a set. She lost in the final, 6–0, 7–5. That same year, at the age of 14, Maria turned professional.

Maria suffered from Osgood-Schlatter's disease. This disease causes a person's legs to grow extremely quickly. That's why Maria grew so tall in such a short time. Because of her illness, Maria's knees often hurt. She couldn't do running drills. Over time, she outgrew the disease.

Maria stretches her long legs during practice.

Soon after, she competed in her first pro tournament at Indian Wells, California. She won her first match. She met the great Monica Seles in the second round. Seles whipped her 6–0, 6–2. "For her age, she's just great!" said Seles. Maria figured she had a long way to go. She said, "Today I learned there is a big difference between a junior and a pro . . . a big difference." The Women's Tennis Association (WTA) **ranked** Maria for the first time. She was number 532.

Maria yells as she makes a shot at the 2003 Australian Open.

MARIA MANIA

In her early pro career, Maria lost before she won. In 2003, she made it to the Australian Open, a Grand Slam event. She lost in the first round. In fact, in each of her next four pro tournaments, she lost in the first round. But Maria didn't sulk. She stayed positive.

Finally, midway through the year in Birmingham, England, she won her first four matches. She reached the **semifinal** round before losing. This performance pushed her to number 88 in the rankings.

At Wimbledon, the oldest Grand Slam event, she reached the third round. She won a match at the US Open. On October 5, 2003, at the age of 16, she won her first tournament in Tokyo, Japan. She was ranked number 33. One month later, she won her second tournament in Quebec, Canada. She was on her way!

Maria *(shown here)* battles Yugoslavia's Jelena Dokic at Wimbledon in 2003.

Maria was loud on the court. She grunted when she hit the ball. On big swings, she screamed. **Opponents** sometimes complained. Maria said she couldn't help it. She got the nickname the Queen of Screams. One person was even louder than Maria—her father. Yuri yelled from the stands and was often warned to quiet down.

Maria winds up for a backhand return to Monica Seles in a 2003 match.

Maria stayed focused on tennis. She started 2004 ranked number 31 in the world. She ended the year at number 4! She got to the third round at the Australian Open. She also reached her first-ever Grand Slam **quarterfinal** at the French Open. "I don't think anything can stop me," she said, "unless I lose."

At Wimbledon, she rolled through the first four rounds. In the semifinals, she beat former champion Lindsay Davenport. "I had control of the match," said Davenport, "and she took it from me."

With her height, blonde hair, and green eyes, Maria looks like a fashion model. Companies have asked her to model for them. She also started to have her tennis outfits specially designed for her.

Serena Williams *(bottom)* watches Maria as she serves at Wimbledon in 2004.

Maria played two-time defending champion Serena Williams in the final. Maria won the first set, 6–1. She trailed 2–4 in the second set. She focused harder. She won four straight games to win the title. Maria could hardly believe it. "I'm on my knees celebrating," she said, "and I'm thinking, 'What have I just done?'" She was the third-youngest champion ever at Wimbledon.

Maria became an instant megastar. Photographers followed her everywhere. She appeared on TV talk shows. Dozens of companies begged her to help sell their products. IMG created Team Sharapova. This group handles her deals and publicity. Maria signed sponsorships with makers of cell phones; cameras; cars; watches; soft drinks; toothpaste; and, of course, tennis rackets. She even had a perfume named after her.

Soon she was earning $22 million a year. She was among the highest-paid female athletes in the world. "I do feel like I'm being pulled in many different directions," said Maria. "It's been amazing. It was hard at first, but I've been enjoying every second of it."

Maria returns a shot to Amelie Mauresmo at a WTA tournament.

BACK TO THE TOP

In 2005, Maria reached the semifinals in three of the four Grand Slams. She also won three titles in other tournaments. In August, she became the number one ranked female tennis player in the world. She was the first female player from Russia to reach number one. "It's a dream come true," she said.

Maria won two 2006 ESPY sports awards. She was named Best International Female Athlete and Best Female Tennis Player.

Shoulder and ankle injuries slowed Maria in 2006. But she still won five tournaments. The biggest was the US Open. Maria faced Justine Henin in the finals. The two had battled each other five times in the past. Henin had won four of those matches. But this time, Maria came out on top, winning both sets 6–4.

Maria felt happy and grateful after her US Open victory. But she knew she was just getting started. "To win your second [Grand Slam], it's kind of like a cherry on the cake," she said. "But there are a lot more cherries that I'm going to put on that cake."

She tried hard to win those extra cherries in 2007. She made it to the final of the Australian Open. But she lost to Serena Williams. In 2008, Maria won match after match and reached the Australian Open final once again. This time, she faced Ana Ivanovic. Maria won the match in two sets, 7–5 and 6–3. She had captured three of the four Grand Slams!

Maria *(shown here)* playing Ana Ivanovic at the Australian Open.

Maria was on top of the tennis world. But her shoulder continued to cause her pain. She had surgery to fix the problem in October 2008. The shoulder had not healed well enough for Maria to play

Maria lets out a scream on the court.

in the 2009 Australian Open. She struggled to regain her form over the next few years. By the end of 2011, Maria was ranked in the top five in the world again.

The Russian tennis star had fully recovered by 2012. She proved her health by finally winning the French Open and completing the career Grand Slam.

Maria is the highest-paid female athlete in the world, according to *Forbes* magazine. She earned about $29 million between June 2012 and June 2013.

An even bigger honor came her way later that year. Maria carried her country's flag at the Opening Ceremony of the Olympic Games in London, England. Then she made it to the women's **singles** finals. She lost to Serena Williams. Maria took home a silver medal.

Maria continues to play at a high level. Late in 2013, she was ranked number 3 in the world. But she has her sights set even higher. "Number one is a great number," she said with a laugh.

Selected Career Highlights

2013 Reached the finals at the French Open

2012 Won the singles title at the French Open to complete career grand slam
Ended the year ranked number 2
Won a silver medal in singles at the Olympic Games

2011 Reached the finals at Wimbledon
Ended the year ranked number 4

2010 Ended the year ranked number 18

2009 Ended the year ranked number 14

2008 Won the singles title at the Australian Open
Ended season early due to shoulder surgery

2007 Reached the singles final of the Australian Open
Reached the semifinals of the French Open
Ended the year ranked number 4

2006 Won the singles title at the US Open
Reached the semifinals at the Australian Open and Wimbledon
Won ESPY for Best Female Tennis Player
Ended the year ranked number 2

2005 Reached the semifinals at the Australian Open, Wimbledon, and the US Open
Ranked number 1 for the first time
Won ESPY for Best Female Tennis Player
Ended the year ranked number 4

2004 Won the singles title at Wimbledon
Named Tour Player of the Year
Named Most Improved Player of the Year
Ended the year ranked number 4

2003 Won first WTA tournament in Tokyo, Japan

2002 Won first professional tournament in Japan

2001 Played first professional tournament

Glossary

ace: a serve that is not returned by the other player

agent: a person or group that an athlete hires to handle the athlete's contracts and publicity

backhand: hitting the ball while holding the racket so that the back of the hand is facing the target

baseline: the line that marks the back end of a tennis court

dormitory: a large building with bedrooms that house many students

final: the round in a singles tournament in which only two players remain

Grand Slam: one of four tennis championships played around the world each year. The events are the Australian Open, the French Open, Wimbledon (in Great Britain), and the US Open.

opponents: other players in a match

professional: being able to play in tournaments for money

quarterfinal: the round in a singles tournament in which eight players remain

ranked: to be given a number based on performance in tennis tournaments. The lower the number is, the better the ranking

returns: shots made in answer to the opponent's serves

semifinal: the round in a singles tournament in which four players remain

serve: the hit of a tennis ball that starts each point in a tennis game

set: in a tennis match, a group of six or more games. Women's tennis matches have a maximum of three sets.

singles: a tennis match that pits one player against another

tournament: a competition in which a series of games determines the winning player

tuition: money paid to a school so a student can be taught there

Further Reading & Websites

Donaldson, Madeline. *Venus & Serena Williams*. Minneapolis: Lerner Publications, 2011.

Egart, Patricia. *Let's Play Tennis! A Guide for Parents and Kids by Andy Ace*. Eagan, MN: Amber Skye Publishing, 2010.

King, Donna. *Game, Set, and Match*. Boston: Kingfisher, 2007.

Maria's Website
http://www.mariasharapova.com
Maria's official website features trivia, photos, records, and information about Maria and the United States Tennis Association.

Sports Illustrated Kids
http://www.sikids.com
The *Sports Illustrated Kids* website covers all sports, including tennis.

United States Tennis Association
http://www.usta.com
The USTA's website provides fans with recent news stories, statistics, schedules, and biographies of players.

Women's Tennis Association
http://www.wtatennis.com
The WTA's website features information about players, tournaments, rules, and rankings.

LERNER
SOURCE

Expand learning beyond the printed book. Download free, complementary educational resources for this book from our website, www.lerneresource.com.

Index

Photo Acknowledgments

The images in this book are used with the permission of: © Clive Brunskill /Getty Images, pp. 4, 5, 7, 18; © Christian Liewig/Liewig Media Sports /CORBIS, p. 6; © Kenzo Trbouillard/AFP/Getty Images, p. 8; © Sergei Ilnitsky /epa/CORBIS, p. 9; © Dean Treml/Getty Images, p. 10; © Art Seitz, pp. 12, 14, 17; AP Photo/Dave Caulkin, p. 19; © Peter Parks/AFP/Getty Images, p. 20; © Michael Cole/CORBIS, p. 22; © Lisa Blumenfeld/Getty Images, p. 24; AP Photo/Mark Baker, p. 26; © Julian Abram Wainwright/epa/CORBIS, p. 27; © Don Emmert/AFP/Getty Images, p. 29.

Front cover: © Matthew Stockman/Getty Images.

Main body text set in Caecilia LT Std 55 Roman 16/28.
Typeface provided by Adobe Systems.